The **Ultimate** Guide to **Cricket**

Gavin Mortimer

This book was conceived, edited and designed for Puffin Books by
Tony Potter Publishing Ltd.
www.tonypotter.com

Editor: **Pat Hegarty**
Illustrators: **John Cooper & Brett Hudson**

With special thanks to **Lucian Clinch**
for his ideas, input and enthusiasm

PUFFIN BOOKS

Published by the Penguin Group
Penguin Books Ltd, 80 Strand, London WC2R 0RL, England
Penguin Group (USA) Inc., 375 Hudson Street, New York, New York 10014, USA
Penguin Group (Canada), 90 Eglinton Avenue East, Suite 700, Toronto, Ontario, Canada M4P 2Y3
(a division of Pearson Penguin Canada Inc.)
Penguin Ireland, 25 St Stephen's Green, Dublin 2, Ireland (a division of Penguin Books Ltd)
Penguin Group (Australia), 250 Camberwell Road, Camberwell, Victoria 3124, Australia
(a division of Pearson Australia Group Pty Ltd)
Penguin Books India Pvt Ltd, 11 Community Centre, Panchsheel Park, New Delhi – 110 017, India
Penguin Group (NZ), cnr Airborne and Rosedale Roads, Albany, Auckland 1310, New Zealand
(a division of Pearson New Zealand Ltd)
Penguin Books (South Africa) (Pty) Ltd, 24 Sturdee Avenue, Rosebank, Johannesburg 2196, South Africa

Penguin Books Ltd, Registered Offices: 80 Strand, London WC2R 0RL, England

www.penguin.com

First published 2006
1

Text copyright © Tony Potter Publishing Ltd, 2006
Illustrations copyright © Tony Potter Publishing Ltd / Getty Images Ltd, 2006
All rights reserved

The moral right of the author and illustrator has been asserted

Made and printed in Dubai

British Library Cataloguing in Publication Data
A CIP catalogue record for this book is available from the British Library

ISBN-13: 978–0–141–32184–4
ISBN-10: 0–141–32184–9

Contents

Opening Shots

Cricket captured the imagination of the world in 2005 with the incredible Ashes series between England and Australia.

All over the world a new generation of fans are being thrilled by the big-hitting batting of **Kevin Pietersen** and **Brian Lara**, and the brilliant bowling of **Shoaib Akhtar** and **Shane Warne**.

This book tells you everything you want to know about cricket. There's the Heaven's XI – an All-Stars team of the world's best, including **Andrew 'Freddie' Flintoff** and **Sachin Tendulkar**. There are plenty of tips on how to swing the ball like England's **Simon Jones** and how to hook a six like **Jacques Kallis** of South Africa.

You'll find the lowdown on the 2007 World Cup and the new and exciting Twenty20 cricket. Test your cricketing knowledge with the Stumped questions throughout the book.

In fact, this book is crammed so full of crazy cricket facts and smashing stats …it'll hit you for six!

Kevin Pietersen smashes another boundary for England at the Oval during their fabulous Ashes win against Australia in September 2005

Michael Vaughan in action

HEAVEN'S XI

All about Heaven's XI

● Look out for this Heaven's XI feature which appears throughout the book. It's a top team put together by our panel of cricket experts. But the great thing about cricket is that no two experts will ever agree! Why not be a cricket team selector and put together your own 'Dream Team'?

It can be made up of today's best players, or you may want to draw from history - don't forget to check out our Historical Heaven's XI feature on Page 56.

Stumped?

Test your cricketing knowledge where you see this logo. If you really are stumped, the answers are on Page 64!

The Global Game

Scotland Cricket began in the 18th Century. Scotland played in its first World Cup in 1999 and has also qualified for the 2007 tournament

Canada Toronto played New York at cricket in 1844, the oldest international fixture, and Canada have appeared in the 1979 and 2003 World Cup Finals.

Ireland Cricket is believed to have been played since the 1700s and Ireland will compete in the 2007 World Cup for the first time.

USA Cricket was first played in the USA in the 1750s and a touring team visited Britain in 1968. There are many clubs on the east and west coasts of America.

England The birthplace of cricket and where a form of the sport was played as early as the 1300s. England first played a Test match in 1877.

Kenya Cricket has been played for over 100 years and in 1996 Kenya beat the West Indies in a World Cup match.

West Indies Cricket began in the early 19th Century and the West Indies played their first Test vs England in 1928.

Fiji The first cricket match was in 1874. Cricket is popular in schools but Fiji has never played a Test match.

Zimbabwe Cricket started in the 1890s when the country was called Rhodesia. In 1981, after independence, it changed to Zimbabwe and its first Test was vs India in 1992

The cricketing map of the world

Cricket is played in every continent of the world, as you can see from this map, which shows you all the cricketing nations. There are many that you would expect to see, such as England and Australia, plus a few that might surprise you, such as Holland and Denmark!

Argentina The first cricket club was established in 1831 but they have not played any Test matches.

Holland The first proper Dutch club was formed in 1855 and Holland competed in the 1996 and 2003 World Cups.

Denmark Cricket has been played since the 1860s and Dane Ole Mortensen played for English side Derbyshire.

United Arab Emirates Cricket has been popular since the early 1980s and in 1996 the UAE played in its first World Cup tournament.

Bangladesh They gained their independence from Pakistan in 1971 and played their first Test vs India in 2000.

Japan Cricket began in the late 19th Century and the sport is becoming popular in some of Japan's universities.

Malaysia The Malaysia Cricket Association was formed in 1963 and the sport is becoming more popular.

Pakistan They played their first Test match in October 1952 against India.

Sri Lanka When cricket was first played here, the country was called Ceylon. Now named Sri Lanka, their first Test was vs England in 1982.

South Africa British soldiers introduced cricket 200 years ago and South Africa's first Test match was vs England in 1889.

India Cricket was first played by British sailors in 1721 and India played England in their first Test match in 1932.

Australia Cricket was first played in the early 19th Century and Australia's first Test match was in 1877 vs England.

New Zealand Cricket has been played in New Zealand since the 1830s but they didn't play their first Test match until 1930 vs England.

Crazy for Cricket

Ten Top of the Order facts that will bowl you over!

1 The laws of cricket were first issued way back in 1744 by the London Club and ever since then the length of a **cricket pitch** has been 22 yards (20 metres).

2 In a Test match against England in 1979, Australian player Dennis Lillee came to the wicket with a metal bat. The English team complained to the umpires that the bat was damaging the ball and Lillee was told to use a **wooden bat**. A law was soon passed banning metal bats.

3 The word 'umpire' comes from the Old French word 'Nompere', which means not equal or not a player in one of the teams. When cricket was first played 500 years ago there was only one umpire, not two as there are today.

4 The 1744 laws stated that an **over** was to be made up of four balls. In 1889 the law was changed, increasing it to five balls and in 1900 it was altered again so that an over contained six balls.

5 When cricket began people bowled underarm but at the start of the 19th Century this changed to overarm. Legend has it that the person responsible for inventing **overarm bowling** was a woman called Christina Willes. She used to bowl to her brother, John but her large skirt prevented her from bowling underarm so she changed to overarm.

6 All batsmen wear **helmets** nowadays to protect their heads but the first batsman to use one in a Test match was Australian Graham Yallop, against the West Indies, in 1978.

7 One of the most famous cricketers ever was England's W. G. Grace. He made his first-class debut in 1865, aged 17 and he carried on playing until he was **60 years old**.

8 W. G. Grace was an 'all-rounder', which means that he could bat and bowl well. There have been many great all-rounders in cricket, although the best was probably Gary Sobers of the West Indies. *(see page 56)*

9 The inside of a cricket ball is made of cork and the outside of leather. The stitches that hold the leather together are called **the seam**. The design of a cricket ball has hardly changed in 300 years, although originally they were white, not red.

10 The headquarters of cricket is at Lord's Cricket Ground in London, named after Thomas Lord who rented some land there in 1787 on which to play cricket.

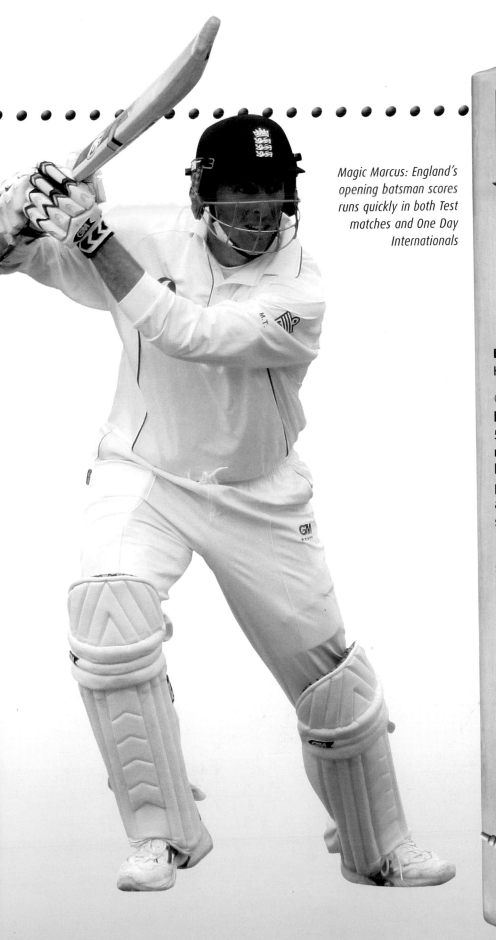

Magic Marcus: England's opening batsman scores runs quickly in both Test matches and One Day Internationals

HEAVEN'S XI

1

Marcus Trescothick
ENGLAND

Born: December 25 1975 in Keynsham, Somerset

- The attacking opening batsman has scored well over 5,000 Test match runs and loves nothing better than striking the ball to the boundary. He first played for England in 2000 against the West Indies and scored 66 in his first innings.

- Trescothick made his highest score of 219 against South Africa in 2003. He has captained England occasionally, especially in One Day International matches.

- He scored 431 runs in the series victory over Australia in 2005 and was awarded the MBE in the same year for his part in helping England win the Ashes.

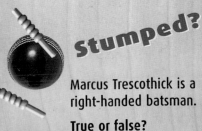

Stumped?

Marcus Trescothick is a right-handed batsman.

True or false?

Do you speak Cricket?

Cricket has a language all of its own which can be confusing when you start playing the game.

Fortunately, the language of cricket is much easier to learn than French or German! Read on to discover all the special lingo that makes cricket such a special sport.

Beamer
A fast delivery that doesn't bounce and reaches the batsman at head height. It's against the laws of cricket.

Bouncer
A fast delivery that bounces once and rises to the batsman's chest or head.

Bump ball
When a batsman hits the ball straight into the ground and it bounces up into the air.

Bye
A run to the batting side that is scored when the batsman leaves the ball and the wicket-keeper misses it.

Duck
When a batsman is out without scoring a run.

Extras
All the runs in a team's total which aren't scored by batsmen. They can be wides, no balls, leg byes or byes.

Fishing
When a batsman tries to play a shot outside his off stump by waving his bat nervously at the ball.

Full toss
A delivery that reaches the batsman without bouncing.

Golden Duck
When a batsman is out to the very first ball he faces.

Googly
A delivery by a right-arm spin bowler to a right-hand batsman that looks as though it will spin towards the off stump, but spins towards the leg stump.

Hat-trick
When a bowler gets three batsmen out with three deliveries, one after another.

Howzat
The loud shout by the bowler to the umpire when he thinks the batsman is out.

LBW
If a batsman is Leg Before Wicket he is out because the ball would have hit the stumps if it hadn't hit the batsman's pads first.

Long Hop
A delivery that is very short and gives the batsman plenty of time to hit it.

Leg Bye
A run awarded to the batting side that is scored when the ball hits the batsman's legs.

Maiden Over
An over in which no runs are scored.

Nightwatchman
One of the batsmen from lower down the order who comes in to bat higher up the order if a wicket falls near the close of a day's play.

No Ball
A run added to the total when the bowler steps over the popping crease and has no part of his foot behind it, before he has let go of the ball.

Non-striker
The batsman who is not facing the bowler.

Over
A bowler bowls six deliveries to the batsman in one over.

Popping crease
A funny name for the line four feet (1.22m) in front of the stumps. The batsman usually stands behind it when he is batting.

Stumps
Each wicket has three wooden stumps with two bails on top. The centre stump is called the 'middle stump', the one closest to the batsman's legs is called the 'leg stump' and the stump closest to the batsman's bat is the 'off stump'.

Tailenders
The last two or three batsmen in a side who aren't as good at batting as the rest of the team.

Twelfth Man
Like a substitute in football, the twelfth man is an extra player who can replace an injured team-mate, although he can't bowl or bat and can only field.

Wide
A run which is added to the total when a delivery is too wide of the stumps for the batsman to have a chance of hitting the ball.

Yorker
A delivery that bounces at the batsman's toes and is very hard to hit.

King of the Swingers

Will it move in or will it move out?

That's the question every batsman asks himself when he faces a swing bowler.

There have been many great swing bowlers over the years. Pakistan's Wasim Akram and Ian Botham of England were two of the best, but the most deadly swing bowler in the 21st Century is **Simon Jones.** He can bend a cricket ball like David Beckham can bend a football!

When England beat Australia in 2005 to win the Ashes, Jones took an awesome 18 wickets in four matches and left the Aussies in a spin because of his amazing swing!

But making a cricket ball swing isn't as easy as it sounds. For a start, the weather makes a difference. If it's hot and sunny, then the ball won't swing that much. But if it's grey and warm, then the ball will swing much more. No one knows for sure why this should be, but it's true. Perhaps this is why the English have so many great swing bowlers - the summer weather is ideal!

A good swing bowler makes every batsman's heart beat a little faster, because it's not easy to play a shot at a ball that is travelling at 80mph, and swinging too!

And there is worse news for the batsmen! There are two types of swing bowlers. There are those that swing the ball into the stumps and those that swing the ball away from the stumps.

Read on to find out how you too can become King of the Swingers for your team…

England's Simon Jones is one of the world's best swing bowlers as he showed against Australia in 2005

How to bowl an inswinger

Imagine you're bowling to a right-handed batsman. Well, an inswinger should move in the air from his off-side to his leg-side. In other words, it should swing in to him. To help the swing, polish one side of the ball on your trousers before each ball to give it some extra shine. Why? Because the polished half of the ball moves through the air more quickly than the unpolished side and so it will swing.

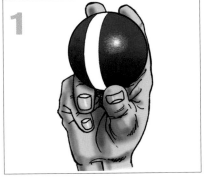

Hold the ball with the seam upright. Place your thumb on the seam underneath the ball and your index and middle fingers either side of the seam at the top of the ball.

With the unpolished side of the ball facing the batsman keep the seam upright but point it towards fine leg *(see page 52 for fielding positions).*

Run in and bowl on a line outside the off stump so that the ball will swing in towards the batsman's off stump. Get ready to shout for an LBW appeal!

How to bowl an outswinger

Now that you can make the ball swing in to the batsman, what about confusing him even more by making it swing away from him?

Grip the ball as for the inswinger with the thumb on the seam underneath the ball and the index and middle fingers either side of the seam above.

But this time point the upright seam towards the slips and make sure the polished side of the ball is facing the batsman.

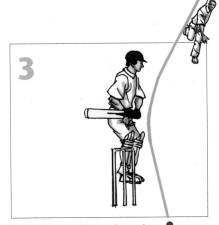

Run in and bowl at the batsman's front pad so that the ball will swing out from him and who knows, this time you might be appealing for a catch behind!

Best of the Tests

Test cricket is full of nerve-tingling excitement as two teams spend five days trying to win the game.

There's been some amazing action in Test matches and here are a few of the best.

There have been only two tied matches since Test cricket began. The first was in 1960, when Australia and the West Indies finished on exactly the same scores, and in 1986 Australia and India tied their match.

The first Test matches in England lasted no more than three days. In 1930 they were increased to four days and in 1948 they became five days.

In other countries Test matches used to have no time limit and in 1939 England played South Africa in Durban in a match that lasted eleven days. The match was only stopped when England had to catch the boat back home!

In his last ever Test match in 1948 Australia's **Don Bradman** needed to score four runs to finish with a Test average of 100. He was out for 0 and so he ended his career with an average of 99.94. Unlucky!

The youngest player ever to play Test cricket is **Hasan Raza** of Pakistan. He made his debut in 1996 against Zimbabwe and had to ask his headteacher for time off school. He was only 14 years and 227 days old!

The only Test match in which three brothers appeared on the same team was in 1880 when **William**, **Edward** and **Fred Grace** all played for England against Australia - and they didn't have one argument!

The youngest ever captain of a Test match side is **Mansoor Ali Khan Pataudi**. When he led India on to the field against the West Indies in 1962 he was only 21 years and 77 days old.

No bowler has ever taken all 20 wickets in one match, but England's **Jim Laker** came very close in 1956 against Australia. In the first innings he dismissed nine Aussies and in the second he got all ten out!

Bangladesh are the tenth and most recent country to play Test match cricket. They played their first Test against India in 2000 and in 2005 they played in England for the first time.

Stumped?

Which two countries played each other in the first ever Test match in 1877?

ENGLAND		TOTAL	273
✱TRSCOTHCK	132	WICKETS	0
—STRAUSS	125	OVERS	85
BUTCHER			
VAUGHAN		BATSMAN ✕	132
THORPE		BATSMAN —	125
FLINTOFF		PARTNERSHIP	273
JONES		RUNS TO WIN	
GILES		OVERS LEFT	15
HOGGARD		RATE ACH'D	3.2
JONES		RATE REQ'D	
HARMISON			

A partnership total of 273 during the second Test between South Africa and England in 2004

*Graeme Smith
in action*

2

Graeme Smith
SOUTH AFRICA

Born: February 1 1981
in Johannesburg

● The tall, left-handed Smith made 68 on his Test debut against South Africa in 2002 and he has continued to score runs ever since.

● In March 2003 he became captain of his country at the age of 22 – South Africa's youngest-ever skipper – and a few months later he scored back-to-back double centuries in the drawn series against England.

● Although he found runs harder to score against India and Sri Lanka in 2004, Smith was in wonderful form playing against the West Indies in 2005. He scored three consecutive Test match centuries and became the first captain of any country since 1977 to tour the West Indies without losing a match.

Stumped?

Graeme Smith captained English side Somerset in 2005.
True or false?

'Catches win Matches'

It's one of the favourite sayings of all cricket coaches – and it's true.

Catches really do win matches. They're just as important as scoring runs or taking wickets. And just like batting and bowling, you can improve your catching by practising.

Catches in a cricket match are all different. Some come off the bat very quickly and if you are fielding close to the batsman you only have a split second to catch the ball. But if you're standing far away on the boundary, the batsman might hit the ball high into the air and you have several seconds to wait before you can catch it.

Shivnarine Chanderpaul of the West Indies waits to take a catch during a match. Notice how he is watching the ball and keeping his hands together

Ten Top Tips to be a cool catcher

1 Always keep your eyes on the ball.

2 Always keep your hands together and near to the body.

3 Keep your arms and hands relaxed and your head still.

4 Get your legs into a comfortable and balanced position.

5 Shout your name if a teammate is near, so that he knows it is your catch.

6 Don't point your fingers upwards towards the ball.

7 Try to catch the ball at eye level.

8 Let the ball come to you, don't reach up for it with your hands.

9 As soon as you have caught the ball, draw your hands into your body.

10 If you're a slip fielder, stand with your knees bent and your hands together waiting for a catch.

Colin Miller of Australia is just about to drop a catch against the West Indies

Look at this photo and write down three reasons why the fielder dropped the catch.

If your answers match those at the bottom of the page, then well done, you're going to be a cool catcher!

Of course, catching a cricket ball is never easy. For a start, it can sometimes hurt! Get your hands used to catching a cricket ball by throwing an old ball from hand to hand. After a while change to a new cricket ball and soon your hands will feel much happier when you're making a catch.

To improve your catching you can throw a ball to a friend. Start by standing five metres apart and then increase the distance to ten metres when you have caught ten balls in a row. Then move 15, 20 and 30 metres apart to really test yourselves.

Tennis balls are also a great way to improve your catching, particularly if all your friends are busy. Stand against a wall (making sure there are no windows nearby!) and throw the ball against it. Then try to catch it before it bounces. See if you can catch 20 in a row without dropping one. Now that really is a cool catcher!

Answers

1. His hands weren't together.

2. His fingers were pointing upwards towards the ball.

3. Look at his feet – he isn't well balanced.

Got all three right? Great! Now ask some friends and see if they can match your score. You could write your own cricket quiz and test your mates.

The Umpire Strikes Back

Umpires are like referees in football or rugby — they make the decisions and ensure the laws of the game are followed.

Unlike most sports, there are two umpires in a cricket match. One stands behind the stumps opposite the batsman who is on strike and the other stands parallel to this batsman.

In this way, the umpires can see everything that is going on. The job of an umpire is very hard because he must make important decisions very quickly, such as whether a batsman is out or a ball is wide. That's why it's important that players always respect the judgement of an umpire.

To let the players, the official scorer and the spectators know what his decisions are during a match, the umpire makes a series of gestures with his arms and legs. If you don't know much about cricket it may seem as though the umpire is dancing!

In fact, each gesture is a special signal with a particular meaning. The most common umpire signals are shown below.

Next time you watch a cricket match, see how many you can spot.

Four runs
When a batsman hits the ball to the boundary.

Six runs
When a batsman hits the ball to the boundary without it bouncing.

Wide ball
When a bowler delivers a ball to the batsman that is too wide to hit.

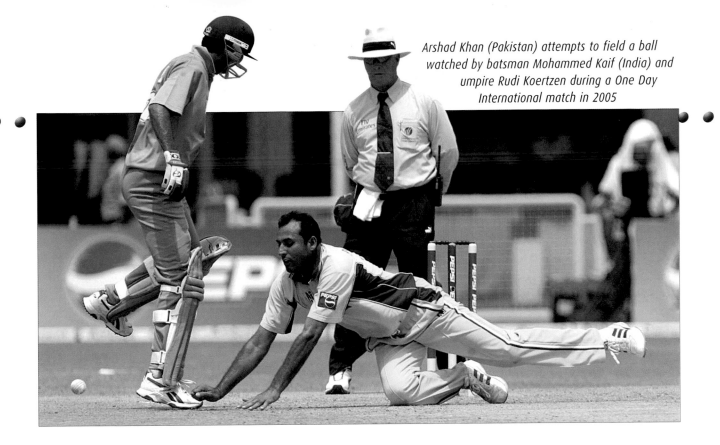

Arshad Khan (Pakistan) attempts to field a ball watched by batsman Mohammed Kaif (India) and umpire Rudi Koertzen during a One Day International match in 2005

No ball
When a bowler puts his whole front foot over the popping crease as he delivers the ball.

Out
When a batsman loses his wicket and is out.

Leg bye
When the ball hits a batsman on the leg and he takes a run.

Over and Out!

One of the reasons why cricket is such a sensational sport is because there are so many ways in which a batsman can be out. Can you figure out the exact number? *(see bottom of page)*

Most batsmen are bowled, caught or LBW, but very occasionally the umpires give a batsman out for bizarre behaviour.

The only batsman out for obstruction in a Test match was England's **Len Hutton**. In a 1951 match he edged a ball from his bat to his pads and the ball spun up in the air. Just as the South African wicketkeeper was going to catch the ball Hutton got in his way and the 'keeper dropped it.

In 1956 **Russell Endean** was the first player given out for handling the ball in a Test when he was batting for South Africa against England. Endean played a defensive shot and then watched in horror as the ball spun back towards his stumps. He flicked it away with his hand and, Howzat!, he was out for handling the ball.

Since then six other batsmen have been given out for using their hands, the most recent being England's **Michael Vaughan** against India in 2001.

And there have been lots of other dramatic dismissals. During the 2005 Ashes, **Shane Warne** stepped back to a ball from **Andrew Flintoff** and trod on his stumps.

But for really bad luck, England's **Kabir Ali** takes the biscuit! He was batting against Pakistan 'A' in 2005 when he thumped a ball back down the wicket. It hit the bat of teammate **Paul Collingwood** at the non-striker's end and bounced up into the air and was caught. The ball hadn't hit the ground so Ali was given out. Kabir is a right-handed batsman from Birmingham, born in 1980. He's played for Worcestershire and was a member of the ECB National Academy.

Shane Warne standing on his stumps in 2005

Hotshot

An umpire cannot give a batsman out unless a member of the fielding team makes an appeal.

Congratulations if you came up with ten. Spot on! A batsman can be out in ten ways: **bowled, caught, hit wicket, LBW** (leg before wicket), **stumped, run out, handled the ball, timed out, obstructing the field** and **hit ball twice.**

20

HEAVEN'S XI

3
Ricky Ponting
AUSTRALIA

Born: December 19 1974 in Tasmania

⚫ The world knew Ricky Ponting was going to be an Aussie ace when he struck a superb 96 on his Test debut against Sri Lanka in 1995. He bats in a very exciting style and scores runs easily in both One Day Internationals and Test matches.

⚫ Ponting was captain of Australia when they won the 2003 World Cup and he smashed an amazing 140 not out in the final against India. If that wasn't bad enough for India, later that same year Ponting scored 257 in one innings against them!

⚫ He played his 100th Test match against South Africa in 2006 and celebrated in awesome style with magnificent centuries in both innings.

Stumped?

Ricky Ponting has taken some wickets in Test Matches as a bowler.
True or false?

The Fab Four

They could just as easily be called the 'Frightening Four' because England's fast-bowling attack is the scariest in the world.

Steve Harmison

Simon Jones

Matthew Hoggard

Andrew Flintoff

Matthew Hoggard shatters the stumps of South Africa's Adam Bacher

Steve Harmison, **Matthew Hoggard**, **Simon Jones** and **Andrew Flintoff** all bowl at over 80 miles per hour and there's nothing they like better than sending the stumps of an opposition batsman flying out of the ground!

What makes the England fast bowlers so dangerous is that each of them has a different skill. Put all of those skills together in a match and the poor batsmen don't stand a chance. Just look at Australia during the 2005 Ashes! England took 85 Aussie wickets in the five Test matches and the Fab Four claimed 75 of them... Howzat for excellence!

Steve Harmison bowls at speeds of over 90 mph

Steve Harmison opens the bowling for England. He's a huge man who bowls the ball from a great height and makes it bounce very high. Oh, and he's quick. Sometimes 'Harmy' bowls at 95mph!

Matthew Hoggard, known to his friends as 'Hoggy', is the slowest of the Fab Four but the man with the long blond hair still bowls at around 80mph. He makes the ball swing a lot so batsmen never know what shot to play.

Andrew Flintoff, nicknamed Freddie, is just as tall as Harmison and nearly as quick! He bowls with amazing aggression and is so accurate he puts pressure on the batsmen.

Simon Jones is nicknamed 'the Racehorse' because he moves as quickly as one when he runs in to bowl! The Welshman swings the ball in and out and makes life very hard for the opposition batsmen.

They certainly are fab and they certainly are fast. And, boy, are they frightening!

Hotshot

Simon Jones is the youngest of the Fab Four and was born on Christmas Day 1978.

Spin to Win

OK, so the fast bowlers are the ones who make a batsman's knees knock together with fear...

But the spinners are the ones who can tie them up in knots with all the clever tricks. There's that wizard Warne, Muralitharan the magician, India's amazing Anil Kumble, and England's Monty Panesar is shaping up to be a winner of a spinner - in his debut for England against India in the first Test in March 2006, he took the wicket of the mighty Sachin Tendulkar. What is their secret? How do spin bowlers make the ball turn so sharply, and in different directions?

There are two main types of spin bowler in cricket. The **leg spinner** and the **off spinner**. Confused? Don't be, it's all very easy to understand – but it might not be as easy to master!!

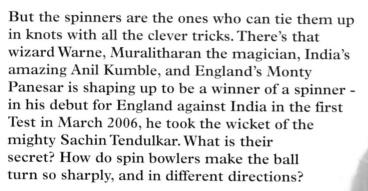

In 2005 against England, Shane Warne of Australia became the first man to take 600 wickets in Test match cricket

Hotshot

Only twice in the history of Test cricket has a bowler dismissed all ten batsmen in one innings. England's **Jim Laker** bowled out Australia in 1956 and **Anil Kumble** of India dismissed ten Pakistani batsman in 1999 – and both were spinners.

Leg spinner

The most famous spin bowler is Australian ace **Shane Warne** and he's a leg spinner. That means when he bowls to a right-handed batsman he makes the ball spin from the leg-side to the off-side. It's the hardest skill to learn but many batsmen find it the hardest spin to play. Warne has spun out over 600 batsmen in his terrific Test career. So here's how to wow 'em like Warney!

1 Hold the ball so that the middle and third finger are at the top with the first joints resting over the seam. The top of the index finger and the thumb rest against the side of the seam.

2 As you bowl the ball, straighten your fingers and use your wrist and your third finger to spin the ball in an anti-clockwise direction.

Off spinner

Off-spin bowlers, like the great **Muttiah Muralitharan** of Sri Lanka, manage to make the ball turn in the other direction from a leg-spinner. Bowled at a right-handed batsman, the ball will spin from the off-side to the leg-side. It might not be as hard an art to master as leg spin, but an awesome off-spinner can make a batsman very blue!

1 Hold the ball firmly with the middle and index fingers on top and across the seam, with the third finger resting against one side and the thumb the other.

2 At the moment you bowl the ball, flick your wrist in a clockwise direction and use your index and middle fingers to spin the ball.

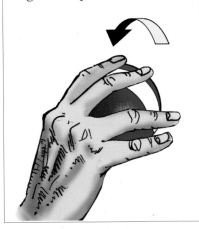

Indian Summer

India has a tradition of producing great batsmen.

They are not necessarily the big-hitting kind who smash sixes all over the ground, but players with style and elegance, capable of playing a wide variety of shots.

Here are some of India's hottest stars:

Vijay Hazare played for India in the 1940s and 1950s and his trademark shot was the cover drive *(see page 50)*. He scored more than 2,000 runs in 30 Test matches.

Another talented batsman for India in the 1950s was **Polly Umrigar**, and he and Hazare helped turn India into a strong cricket side.

Then in the late 1960s two young players appeared who were incredible. **Gundappa Viswanath** first played for India in 1969.

He was out for a duck in his first innings against Australia but in the second innings he scored a fabulous 137.

In 1971 **Sunil Gavaskar** played the first of 125 Test matches for India. When he retired in 1987 he had scored an amazing 10,122 runs at an average of 51.12.

But in the last few years India have been lucky enough to find several other batsmen just as good as Gavaskar.

Sachin Tendulkar has now scored more runs than Gavaskar and players like **Rahul Dravid**, **Virender Sehwag** and **VVS Laxman** are brilliant batsmen who score plenty of runs and make India very hard to beat.

Sunil Gavaskar scored 34 centuries for India in Test matches

Rahul Dravid scored 270 against Pakistan in 2004

Sachin Tendulkar in action

HEAVEN'S XI

4
Sachin Tendulkar
INDIA

Born April 24 1973 in Mumbai, India

🌑 Tendulkar was only 16 years old when he played his first Test match for India. It was against Pakistan in 1989 and although he was cracked on the head by a fast ball he bravely batted on.

🌑 Since then he has scored well over 10,000 Test runs, more than any other Indian batsman. He had an outstanding season in 2004 when he scored 241 against Australia and then, later in the year, he smashed an unbeaten 248 to help India to victory over Bangladesh.

🌑 Tendulkar is also superb for India in One Day Internationals and has been Man of the Match more than 50 times.

Stumped?

In his first One Day International Tendulkar was out for 0.
True or false?

The Ashes

For a joke, somebody put a notice in a newspaper announcing that English cricket had died and the body would be cremated with the ashes taken to Australia.

Of course there weren't really ashes - it was just a joke - but in the winter of 1882 an English team visited Australia to play some matches. England won the series and to celebrate they burned a stump and brought the ashes back to England in an urn. Ever since then the two sides have played each other, not for a big silver cup, but for a small urn of ashes. Australia have won 127 of the 311 Ashes matches with England triumphant in 96 and there have been many unforgettable series.

England lifted the Ashes in 1932/33 using a tactic called Bodyline. Their very fast bowlers bowled at the heads of the Australians – and remember, this was before batsmen wore helmets. It caused a lot of controversy, and a lot of bruises!

Australia had their revenge in 1948 when they won the Ashes in England and didn't lose a single match during the whole tour. The most thrilling Ashes series before 2005 was in 1981 when Ian Botham inspired England to success with some magical displays of batting and bowling.

England roared to victory in the Ashes in 2005 after a series of nail-biting matches against Australia. But do you know how the 'Ashes' got their strange name?

The answer lies way back in history. In 1882 Australia beat England by just seven runs in an exciting match at the Oval in London.

*Ian Botham attacks
Australia in 1981*

Fant'ash'tic Facts

Sydney Gregory of Australia played in a record 52 Ashes matches between 1890 and 1912, a feat that will probably never be beaten as the two countries don't play each other as often now as they did in the early years. Now England and Australia play for the Ashes every two years and play the other countries in between.

The Australian **Allan Border** captained his country in a record 29 Ashes matches, more than any other skipper from either Australia or England.

Kevin Pietersen thumped seven sixes in the second innings of the 2005 Oval Test to set a new record for the most sixes hit in one Ashes innings.

The lowest score made by an Australian side in an Ashes innings was 36 all out in 1902. England's worst score of 45 occurred in 1887.

The highest ever score in an Ashes innings was made by England in 1938. They scored an incredible 903 runs for the loss of only seven wickets with **Len Hutton** making 364!

The original Ashes urn is on display at Lord's cricket ground and is never removed because it is so fragile.

The great Australian batsman **Don Bradman** has scored more runs in Ashes matches than anyone else. His 5,028 runs came in only 63 innings at an average of 89. Very impressive!!

Only eight bowlers have taken hat-tricks in Ashes matches – four Aussies and four Englishmen. The last to do so was England's **Darren Gough** in 1999.

England celebrate winning the 2005 Ashes

The Stroke Makers

The Hook Shot

If you're a batsman there are few things in cricket that feel as thrilling as hooking a ball over the boundary ropes.

However, if you're a bowler there are few things more upsetting than having one of your balls hooked right out of the ground!

As you can see from this dazzling photo of South Africa's **Jacques Kallis** in action, the hook shot is probably cricket's most spectacular stroke.

But it's also one of the most risky because the hook shot is played when the ball has bounced to the height of your chest or head.

That makes the hook a hard shot to keep down and if you don't hit it quite right you may be caught by a fielder on the boundary.

On the other hand, if you do hit it right, the ball will go flying over the boundary and you'll have the satisfaction of seeing the umpire raise both hands in the air and signal 'six'. Fantastic!

Jacques Kallis playing the hook shot

So how do you play the perfect hook shot? Read on and you'll find out...

Hotshot

The pull shot is similar to the hook, but the pull is played to a ball that only bounces around waist height. So it's easier to roll the wrists and keep the ball low on the ground.

30

1 As soon as you see the ball has bounced short, move your rear foot back and slightly to off stump holding your bat in the backlift.

2 Move your front foot back and slightly to the leg stump so that your back shoulder is now facing the bowler and keep your eyes on the ball.

Look at the photo *(opposite)* of Jacques Kallis hooking the ball. See how he is watching the ball and how he's balanced on the back foot. This allows him to swing his upper body round and really hit the ball hard, high and long. Bye-bye ball!

3 With the weight on your back foot, swing the bat across your chest with the arms fully extended and aim to hit the ball over square leg. Make sure that you follow through with your feet so that once you have hooked the ball they are pointing in the direction of the ball.

Match Abandoned

Cricket is a summer sport - but that doesn't mean the sun always shines!

Rain is cricket's greatest enemy and often stops matches, like this one in Johannesburg in 2005 between South Africa and England

Hail stopped this match between Australia and South Africa in Sydney in 2002

Rain can often stop matches, not just in England, but in Australia, South Africa and all over the world.

The first ever Test match to be abandoned because of heavy rain, without a ball being bowled was England versus Australia at Manchester in 1890. So you see, rain has been around for a long time!

And it's not just rain that is a nuisance to cricketers. Hail stones are a hazard – unless you're a batsman wearing a helmet! – and, believe it or not, it's even been known to snow during cricket matches.

June is normally known for its baking sun, but in 1975 a blizzard stopped play between Lancashire and Derbyshire in Buxton – on June 2! Amazingly, the two teams waited for the snow to melt and then continued the cricket match, which Lancashire won.

Although the sun is much stronger in Australia and India than it is in England, it sometimes gets very hot during the English cricket season.

In 1868 a match between Surrey and Lancashire at the Oval was stopped for an hour because the heat was so great.

So make sure you always put on sun protection cream when you play cricket, and drink lots of water, no matter where you are in the world. Even a weak sun can burn!

Probably the most extraordinary reason for a cricket match being stopped was in Lahore in India in 1937. England were playing India when suddenly the ground began to shake beneath the players' feet. It was an earthquake and so both teams waited in the pavilion until it was safe to resume the game!

Brian Lara in action

5

Brian Lara
WEST INDIES

Born May 2 1969 in Trinidad

● The most famous cricketer of recent years is the West Indies' Brian Lara. Ever since he made his Test debut in 1990 he has thrilled spectators with his brilliant and powerful batting.

● He has scored more runs than any other West Indian and a lot of them have been at England's expense! In 1994 he whacked the English bowlers all over the ground as he scored 375 to set a new record for the most Test runs scored in one innings.

● In 2004 Lara became the first batsman to score 400 runs in a Test innings – and again it was against England!

Stumped?

In 1994 Lara scored a record 501 in one innings playing for English county side Warwickshire.

True or false?

Enhance your Stance

Until you've got to grips with your bat, then thumping a four or smashing a six will be almost impossible.

The way in which a cricketer holds the bat is called the 'grip' and how he stands in front of the stumps waiting for the bowler is called the 'stance'.

The Grip

If you are right-handed, hold the bat handle near the top with the left hand above and the right hand below (do this the other way round if you are left-handed).

Your hands should be close together. Remember not to grip the handle too tightly with your bottom hand or else you will hit the ball up into the air – to a cool catcher on the other team!

The 'V'

You can tell if your grip is good by checking if there is a letter 'V' running down the centre of the handle when you hold it. This 'V' is made by the space between your thumb and second finger when you grip the bat.

Does this grip feel good? If it does, great, go and thump a four! If it doesn't, change it a little bit until you feel comfortable holding the bat. The most important thing is to feel in charge of the bat, so getting your grip right is vital.

Now you've got the grip, let's enhance your stance...

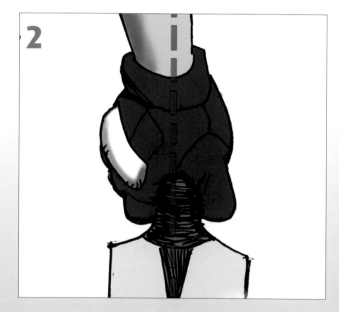

When it comes to your stance, balance is best. Remember that! If you are off balance when you try to play a shot, it won't be a good one.

With your good grip, stand on the balls of your feet with your legs comfortably apart and your knees a little bit bent. Make sure that your front shoulder is pointing at the stumps at the other end and keep your head nice and still.

Hold the bat so that your front hand is resting against your front thigh and the bottom of the bat is grounded behind the toes of your back foot.

Just as the bowler is about to release the ball, lift your bat – not straight back but angled towards second slip. Then as the ball comes towards you, bring your bat back down in a straight line and play the ball.

Look at Andrew Flintoff's stance.
What do you notice about it?

▶ See how he lifts back his bat at a slight angle
▶ See how he keeps his head still as he watches the ball.
▶ See the 'V' shape made by his bottom hand.

Andrew Flintoff has the perfect stance. He trains very hard - remember that practice makes perfect. See if you can match his positioning!

35

Wonder Women

One of the great things about cricket is that everyone can play: young and old, tall and short, boys and girls.

In schools all around the world girls play cricket, but did you know that the very first women's cricket match took place way back in 1745, between Bramley and Hambledon in England?

It took time before the first women's Test match was staged, but finally in 1934 England played Australia in three Test matches that each lasted three days.

England won the first two and the third was drawn.

England also triumphed in the first women's World Cup in 1973, but since then Australia have won the cup five times and in 2005 they beat India in the final.

Women's teams from Australia and England also play for the Ashes, like the men, and in 2005 England's women beat Australia in a Test series for the first time in 42 years to win the Ashes.

Women play cricket all over the world, from England to Australia, from the West Indies to South Africa and from New Zealand to India, and there are lots of fantastic players.

England's **Katherine Brunt** is a fast bowler who frightens lots of batters with her deadly deliveries! She took nine wickets in one match against Australia.

England's captain, **Clare Connor** is an awesome all-rounder who can bat and bowl.

Belinda Clark led Australia to victory in the 2005 World Cup

New to the team is spinner **Holly Colvin,** who made her debut in 2005 aged just 15!

India have some great batters in their side and captain **Mithali Raj** is simply sensational. When India won the Asia Cup in 2006, she cracked a glorious century in the final against Sri Lanka.

Nadine George of the West Indies is also a brilliant batter.

The best in the world is **Karen Rolton** of Australia. She just can't help scoring runs no matter who she plays.

Her top Test score is 209 and when Australia won the World Cup she smashed a spectacular 107.

What a wonder woman!

England celebrate beating Australia in 2005

Caribbean Quickies

The West Indies is a group of islands in the Caribbean where the people are all crazy about cricket!

The West Indies are famous for their quick bowlers, who have been scaring batsmen for years.

In 1959 **Wes Hall** became the first West Indian bowler to take a hat-trick in a Test when he dismissed three Pakistan batsmen in three balls. Hall and **Charlie Griffith** took lots of wickets during the 1960s. In the 1970s the West Indies were bowling quicker than ever and **Michael Holding** was the quickest. In one innings against England in 1976 he took five wickets for only 17 runs. But it wasn't only Holding who made life hairy for batsmen! There was also **Andy Roberts**, **Colin Croft** and **Joel Garner.** Joel Garner was a giant man, 6ft 8in tall, who bowled from such a great height that the ball bounced very awkwardly for the batsmen. In the 1980s and 1990s the West Indies quickies continued. **Malcolm Marshall** was not only very quick but he was deadly accurate. He took 376 wickets in 81 Tests. **Courtney Walsh** and **Curtley Ambrose** played a combined total of 230 Tests and took an incredible 924 wickets between them.

The West Indies need to find some new quickies and perhaps **Jermaine Lawson** is the answer. In 2003 he took a hat-trick of wickets against Australia – when he was only 21!

Michael Holding took 249 wickets in 60 Test matches

Joel Garner in action

Hotshot

Courtney Walsh was brilliant with the ball but bad with the bat - he scored 43 ducks in Test matches!

Pietersen just gets home!

HEAVEN'S XI

6

Kevin Pietersen
ENGLAND

Born: June 27 1980 in Natal, South Africa

● Everything about England's Kevin Pietersen is big! His height, his hitting and his mouth! He stands a massive 6ft 4in and was born in South Africa but because he has an English mother he can play for England.

● Pietersen is famous for his hilarious haircuts and for saying what he thinks. But most of all, Pietersen is famous for his brilliant batting.

● He first played for England in a One Day International against Zimbabwe in 2004 and in 2005 he made his Test debut against Australia.

● He scored 57 in his first innings for England and hit a magnificent 158 in the last Test at The Oval when England won the Ashes.

Stumped?

Pietersen broke his leg playing in a cricket match in 2002. **True or false?**

The Stroke Makers

The forward defensive shot is a very useful tactic

All batsmen love to score runs but that can't happen every ball. When you've just come in to bat, it's best to spend a few balls getting used to the pace of the pitch and the skill of the bowler.

Is he swinging the ball? Is he spinning it? And which way?

So instead of trying to smash a six straight away, play it nice and cool.

The forward defensive shot is great for blocking a ball that is straight and well pitched up – that means it bounces just in front of you so you have to play a shot.

Hotshot:
New Zealand's **Geoff Allott** is a great defensive batsman – in 1999 against South Africa he batted for a record 101 minutes without scoring a run!

Stephen Fleming playing a forward defensive shot

Three steps to learn how to play the defensive shot

With your bat in the backlift position, take a step down the wicket with your front foot towards where the ball is going to pitch. You should be leaning forward slightly with your head and front shoulder, making sure you keep them in line with the ball.

Keep the back leg as straight as possible and as the ball approaches, bend the knee of the front leg as this will help to keep the ball down. Don't take your eyes off of the ball.

Bring the bat down so that it is in front of your pads and keep it straight while you hold the position. Remember that the aim is to block the ball and not to hit it for four.

Learn from the masters

Look at the picture *(opposite)* of New Zealand batsman Stephen Fleming just about to play a forward defensive shot. You can even see the ball as it flies towards his bat! Notice how he is leaning into the shot with his body to keep the ball down when it hits his bat. And see how he's not trying to hit the ball, he's just blocking it.

Record Breakers

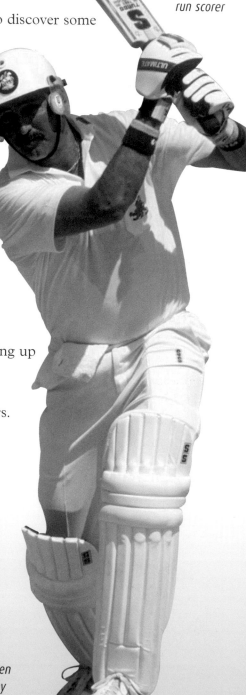

Things can get broken in cricket...

Graham Gooch is England's highest run scorer

Sometimes the bat, sometimes a stump, occasionally a window!

But the one thing every player likes to break is records. Read on to discover some of cricket's remarkable records.

● Australian spinner **Shane Warne** was the first bowler to take 600 Test wickets, but did you know that his teammate **Glen McGrath** has taken more Test wickets than any other fast bowler? But West Indies wizard **Malcolm Marshall** rates as the best Test bowler ever. He took a wicket for every 20.95 runs scored off his bowling.

● **Brian Lara** has scored well over 11,000 Test match runs, which is more than any other batsman, and he's one of only two players to score two triple centuries. Australia's **Don Bradman** is the other and he has the best batting average ever – an amazing 99.94 runs per innings!

● **Graham Gooch** has scored the most runs for England with 8,900 in 118 Tests. **Marcus Trescothick** might be the man to overtake him in the next few years.

● The quickest Test hundred was smashed by West Indies' **Viv Richards** in 1986 against England. He needed only 56 balls to bring up his ton!

● The slowest Test hundred was scored by **Mudassar Nazar** for Pakistan against England in 1978. It took him nine and a half hours. ZZZzzzzzzz!!

Glen McGrath has taken more wickets than any other fast bowler

One Day International matches have their own set of records – and they're always being broken by brilliant batsmen and bowlers!

Saeed Anwar of Pakistan holds the record for the biggest score by a batsman – his massive 194 scored against India in 1997 included 22 fours and 5 sixes.

Another powerhouse Pakistani holds the record for the fastest hundred. **Shahid Afridi** took only 37 balls to smash a century against Sri Lanka in 1996.

And guess what? The first bowler to take 500 wickets in One Day Internationals was also from Pakistan – **Wasim Akram**, who dismissed 502 batsmen in 356 matches.

But the record for the best bowling in a One Day match belongs to **Chaminda Vaas** of Sri Lanka. Playing against Zimbabwe in 2001 he took eight wickets for only 19 runs.

Zimbabwe don't have much luck against Sri Lanka because in a 2004 match they were all out for 35 – a record low score.

And if it's a cool catcher you want, look no further than India's **Mohammad Azharuddin**. He took 156 catches in One Day Internationals – a record he won't drop easily!

The amazing Saeed Anwar in action

Hotshot:
Don Bradman took five runs from a single shot seven times in his career.

Run for your Life

A really good batsman is one who can run.

Watch **Sachin Tendulkar** or **Marcus Trescothick** and see how quickly they sprint up and down the wicket to make sure they get as many runs as they can.

The key to running between the wickets isn't how fast you are, but how well you talk to your batting partner (the non-striker). If you hit the ball in front of you and think you can score a run shout 'Yes' and start to run. Your partner will follow your command and run too.

If you hit the ball to a fielder shout 'No'. If you hit the ball and it goes close to a fielder, shout 'Wait'. Then if the fielder misses the ball you can shout 'Yes' or if he stops it, you shout 'No'.

If you hit the ball behind you it's the non-striker who shouts 'Yes', 'No' or 'Wait' because he can see where the ball is and you can't.

It's important that the non-striker 'backs up' as the bowler comes in to bowl. Backing up means that you don't just stand still watching the ball, but you take a couple of steps down the wicket. But you must remember to keep your bat in the crease, otherwise the bowler can run you out!

England's Andrew Strauss is watching the ball as he runs

Don't forget to watch the ball when you run because you might be able to get a second, a third or even a fourth run – and tell your partner if you think there's another run to be had.

44

HEAVEN'S XI

7

Andrew Flintoff
ENGLAND

Born: December 6 1977 in Preston, England

Andrew Flintoff – better known by his nickname of 'Freddie' – is the world's best all-round cricketer. When he bats he often hits the ball hard and high and he bowls with both pace and accuracy.

Flintoff played his first Test for England in 1998 when he was 20 but he found international cricket tough and struggled to do well. Yet he practised very hard and had his reward in 2002 when he scored his first Test century against New Zealand.

Since then he has got better and better and he was voted England's 'Man of the Series' against Australia in 2005, having scored over 400 runs, smashed 11 sixes and taken 24 wickets. Fantastic Freddie!

Andrew Flintoff scores again!

Stumped?

Flintoff plays cricket in England for Yorkshire. True or false?

The World Cup

The most colourful competition in cricket is the World Cup.

It's held every four years in a different country and it brings together the best players from around the world.

The first World Cup took place in England in 1975. Eight countries competed and the West Indies beat Australia in the final.

Clive Lloyd's West Indies won the cup in 1975 and 1979

Four years later and the West Indies lifted the trophy again, thanks to a hard-hitting hundred from **Viv Richards** and five wickets from **Joel Garner** against England. But in 1983 India beat the West Indies to become champions in a low-scoring match at Lord's. The 1987 World Cup was held in India and Pakistan and the final was between Australia and England.

In a nerve-wracking match in front of 70,000 fans, Australia sneaked home by seven runs despite a fine 58 from England's **Bill Athey**.

In 1992 it was Pakistan who stole the show with fast bowler **Wasim Akram** (below) taking three wickets and hitting 33 in the win over England in the final.

Sri Lanka were the surprise champions in 1996 when they beat Australia in the final after **Aravinda de Silva** scored a sizzling century.

But Australia bounced back in 1999, thrashing Pakistan in the final, and they won again in 2003 after **Ricky Ponting** and **Damien Martyn** destroyed the Indian bowling with a superb stand of 234.

The next World Cup is in 2007 and for the first time it will be held in the West Indies. There will be 16 teams taking part – which is twice as many as competed in the very first World Cup in 1975. Bermuda and Ireland will be playing in their first World Cup.

Damien Martyn (left) and Ricky Ponting were the heroes in the 2003 final

Hotshot:

Pakistan's Wasim Akram holds two World Cup records: he played in a record 38 matches and his 55 wickets are the most taken in the history of the tournament

Keepers aren't Sleepers

There's one position in the fielding team that requires 100 per cent focus - the wicketkeeper.

There's no chance of the wicketkeeper having a quick snooze during a match because he has to concentrate on every ball. He may be diving for a catch, trying to stump out a batsman or perhaps he's taking a throw from a fielder to stop a quick run.

Have you got fantastic focus? If you think you have then perhaps the wicketkeeper is the position for you. You have to be able to catch really well – even though you will wear big gloves – and you need reflexes as fast as a cat!

Adam Gilchrist stumps South Africa's AB de Villiers

Pakistan's Kamran Akmal shows great reflexes to catch Marcus Trescothick of England

1 The position for the wicketkeeper is crouching down with knees bent and gloves together. You should be just outside off stump so that you can see the bowler clearly.

2 As the ball comes down the pitch, rise up and move your body in line with the ball.

3 If the ball bounces below chest height, catch it with the fingers of your gloves pointing down but if it's higher you'll catch it with the fingers pointing horizontally or upwards.

Adam Gilchrist

HEAVEN'S XI

8

Adam Gilchrist
AUSTRALIA

Born: November 14 1971 in Bellingen, Australia

● No other wicketkeeper in the world can bat as brilliantly as Adam Gilchrist.

● He played his first One Day match for Australia in 1996 and three years later made his Test debut against Pakistan. And what a dynamic debut it was! He smashed a superb 81, held five catches and stumped a batsman.

● In Test cricket he usually bats in the middle order but in One Day matches he opens the batting for his side.

● His top score in Tests is 204 and he averages about 50 an innings, which is better than any other 'keeper in history.

● In One Day Internationals Gilchrist has dismissed more batsmen than anyone else by catching or stumping them. For the opposition he really does spell double trouble!

Stumped?

Adam Gilchrist has bowled in a Test match? **True or false?**

The Stroke Makers

The Cover Drive

The cover drive is a classic cricket shot. It's not as dramatic as a hooked six or a square cut for four, but a well-timed drive for four can drive a bowler crazy!

The key to being a demon driver isn't power, although when **Andrew Flintoff** drives he drills it so hard it scorches the grass! Timing is more important than power.

Think about **Brian Lara.** He's not a big man but when he drives the ball it races to the boundary because he has hit the ball with his bat at exactly the right moment.

The cover drive is so-called because you hit the ball on the off side through the covers. Read on to find out how you can become a lover of the cover drive…!

Michael Vaughan
cover driving

Hotshot:
Michael Vaughan was first spotted by the Yorkshire coach when, as a young boy, he was batting on the outfield during the tea interval of a match.

50

Cover drive King

England captain **Michael Vaughan** is known as a great driver of the ball and you will be able to see why from the photograph opposite.

Look carefully at the photo. This picture shows four reasons why Vaughan is a demon driver.

1 His bat is kept in line with his body and it's followed through to the perfect height.

2 His front foot is well forward and his back foot is raised on to its toes.

3 His head is still and his eyes are following the ball.

4 His top hand is controlling the shot so that the ball stays low and doesn't go up in the air.

1 As the ball approaches, step forward to where it will pitch with your front leg and keep the knee slightly bent.

2 Watch the ball carefully and get your head in front of your pads and over the ball as you bring the bat down in a straight line.

3 Holding the bat with a firm top hand and a relaxed bottom hand hit through the ball so that you finish the stroke with the bat face pointing upwards. Lift the back foot on to its toes to help you keep your balance.

51

Fielding Positions

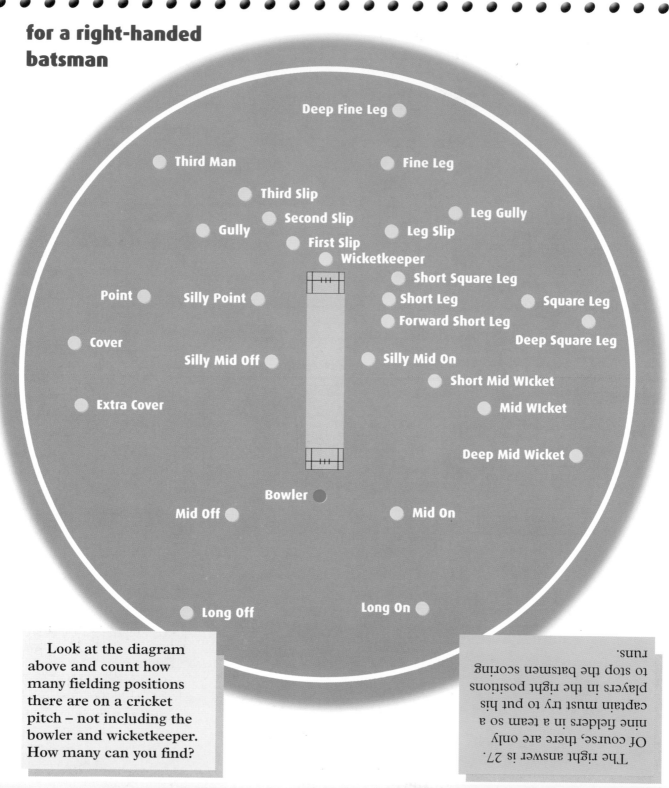

Deep Fine Leg

Third Man   Fine Leg

Third Slip

Second Slip   Leg Gully

Gully   Leg Slip

First Slip

Wicketkeeper

Short Square Leg

Point   Silly Point   Short Leg   Square Leg

Forward Short Leg

Deep Square Leg

Cover

Silly Mid Off   Silly Mid On

Short Mid WIcket

Extra Cover   Mid WIcket

Deep Mid Wicket

Bowler

Mid Off   Mid On

Long Off   Long On

Look at the diagram above and count how many fielding positions there are on a cricket pitch – not including the bowler and wicketkeeper. How many can you find?

The right answer is 27. Of course, there are only nine fielders in a team so a captain must try to put his players in the right positions to stop the batsmen scoring runs.

Some fielders play better in one position than others. For example, Stephen Fleming of New Zealand is a super slip fielder who has caught over 100 batsmen because of his quick reflexes.

When teams play England, batsmen never run a quick single when they hit the ball near Paul Collingwood in the covers because they don't want to be run out. Not only is he quick to pick up the ball but when he throws it at the stumps he usually hits them!

England's Shaun Udal saves four runs with a flying leap

If you are fielding and the ball is hit towards you, don't try to stop it like the fielder in box 1, but turn your body and drop to one knee forming a barrier with your leg as in box 2. Always keep your eyes on the ball!

Turn yourself into a feared fielder by remembering these two top tips:

- Concentrate on every ball. Slip fielders should crouch down and have their hands in the catching position as the bowler bowls. Fielders standing further out should walk in a couple of steps so that they are ready to react if the ball is hit towards them.

- Never give up chasing a ball until it has crossed the boundary rope! Who knows, like Shaun Udal (above), you might stop a four and win the match for your side. Then you'll be a feared and famous fielder!

53

Twenty20 is Tops

Twenty20 cricket is the newest form of cricket and it's tops for thrills!

Somerset celebrate winnng England's Twenty20 Cup in 2005

It started in England in 2003 and has now spread around the world. There are Twenty20 competitions in Australia, the USA, South Africa and New Zealand, and there are even international Twenty20 matches played.

It's called Twenty20 because each side has only 20 overs to hit as many runs as possible, so that means batsmen must do some big hitting and bowlers must get some quick wickets.

With so few overs in which to score runs, some batsmen have invented special shots to help them score as many runs as they can. One of these is called '**The Paddle'.** This is when the batsman hits the ball over the wicket-keeper's head for four runs. There are also special rules for Twenty20 cricket. Did you know that each time a wicket falls, the next batsman must be at the crease within 90 seconds? If he's too slow he is 'timed out' – so he's out before he has even faced a ball!

The Paddle Shot

Shane Warne lets fly

Hotshot:

The first Twenty20 international was in 2005 when Australia beat New Zealand.

HEAVEN'S XI

9

Shane Warne
AUSTRALIA

Born: September 13 1969 in Victoria, Australia

● Spinning sensation Shane Warne is one of the best bowlers in the history of cricket and in 2000 he was voted one of the top five cricketers of all time. In 2005 he became the first bowler ever to take 600 Test wickets and his legendary leg-spin has been tying batsmen in knots for many years!

● In 1994 he took his best match figures of 12 wickets for 128 runs against South Africa. Playing against England in 2005 he was almost as deadly, finishing the series with 40 wickets, which was more than any other bowler on either side. The blond-haired bowler can also bat well and he has scored more than 3,000 runs in Test matches.

● In Test cricket the ball is red, but in Twenty20 cricket a white ball is used because a lot of matches are played in the evening under floodlights and it's much easier to see a white ball than a red ball under the lights.

● Unlike a lot of cricket matches, Twenty20 games only last for three hours, so it's great fun for all the family. If you want to find out more, click on this cricket link: http://www.thetwenty20 cup.co.uk/

Stumped?

Warne's highest score in Test Matches is 99?

True or false?

55

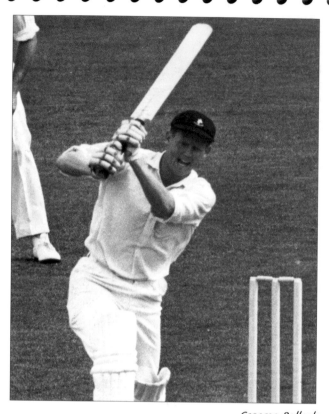

Graeme Pollock

Don Bradman

1 Jack Hobbs (England)
The Englishman scored 62,237 first-class runs in a career that lasted from 1905 to 1934, a record total that still hasn't been beaten. Hobbs played the last of his 61 Tests for England when he was 47.

2 Sunil Gavaskar (India)
Sunil Gavaskar wasn't a spectacular batsman but he always scored runs and was very hard to get out during his Test career which lasted from 1971 to 1987. He was the first batsman to score over 10,000 runs in Test matches.

3 Don Bradman (Australia)
Don Bradman is the best batsman ever and his average of 99.94 runs per Test match innings is an incredible record that will probably never be beaten. He first played for Australia in 1928 and continued to score runs until he retired twenty years later.

4 Graeme Pollock
(South Africa)
Pollock was one of the greatest left-handed batsmen in history. Although he only played 23 Tests in the 1960s, he scored 2,256 runs, at an average of 60 each innings. He once scored an amazing 274 for South Africa against Australia.

5 Ian Botham (England)
England's awesome all-rounder Ian Botham was the first player to score 3,000 runs and take 300 wickets in Test matches. A superb swing bowler and an attacking batsman, Botham played 102 Tests for England between 1977 and 1992.

6 Gary Sobers (West Indies)
The West Indies all-rounder played in 93 Tests between 1954 and 1974, scoring over 8,032 runs and taking 235 wickets. Playing for Nottinghamshire against Glamorgan in 1968 he became the first batsman to hit six sixes in one over.

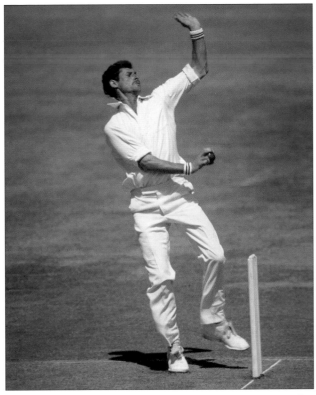

Richard Hadlee

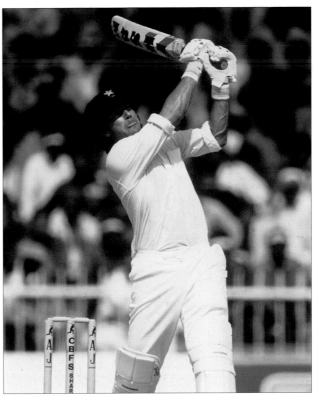

Imran Khan

7 Rod Marsh (Australia)
Rod Marsh played for Australia in the 1970s and 1980s. In 96 Tests he took 343 catches and made 12 stumpings, a world record at that time. He was also a good batsman and was the first Australia wicketkeeper to score a Test century.

8 Richard Hadlee
(New Zealand)
Richard Hadlee was a really tremendous all-rounder who bowled New Zealand to their first ever victory against England in 1978. He took 431 wickets in Test matches and also hit 3,124 runs with a top score of 151.

9 Imran Khan (Pakistan)
Imran Khan is Pakistan's greatest ever cricketer who could bat nearly as well as he could bowl. He was captain for many of his 88 Test matches and in 1987 he led Pakistan to their first ever series win in England.

10 Malcolm Marshall
(West Indies)
The small West Indian was not only a very fast bowler but he could swing the ball both ways and was always bang on target! He played 81 Tests between 1978 and 1991 and took 376 wickets with a best of 7 for 22 against England in 1988.

11 Jim Laker (England)
Jim Laker was a spinner whose off-break bowling claimed 193 wickets in just 46 Test matches. He is best remembered for the 19 wickets he took in a Test against Australia in 1956, but he once bowled out eight batsmen for just two runs!

How the Bat got Fat!

The cricket bat that Andrew Flintoff uses to wallop the ball all over the ground is a whole lot different to the bat which was first used 300 years ago. 'Freddie' might have found it harder to hit a six with one of the early, curved bats!

It looks more like a hockey stick than a cricket bat, doesn't it? That's because back then they bowled underarm so batsmen needed a bat that was heavy at the bottom. But when people started bowling overarm in the 1780s the bat became lighter and straighter because the ball bounced higher.

In the early days, bats were made of one piece of willow wood but as bowling became faster, bats began to break more so makers started to use a piece of cane wood for the handle, with a rubber grip. That was in the 1850s and since then the design of the cricket bat has hardly changed. English white willow is still used because it is a tough and long-lasting wood.

The key to choosing a new bat is whether you feel comfortable holding it. Make sure it's not too heavy or too light. When you've got it home, remember to 'knock it in'. Take an old soft cricket ball and gently bounce it on the face of the bat for a while. Do the same the next day with a wooden mallet and only then will your bat be ready to face the new ball!

A new bat is made for Andrew Flintoff

Hotshot:
In 1835 the length of a bat was restricted to 38 inches (96cm) and this remains the rule today.

Shoaib Akhtar demonstrating his deadly bowling

10

Shoaib Akhtar
PAKISTAN

Born: August 13 1975 in Rawalpindi, Pakistan

When Shoaib Akhtar first roared on to the international cricket scene in 1999 he was the fastest bowler the world had ever seen. He came close to bowling at 100 miles per hour and took lots of wickets.

In a One Day International against New Zealand in 2002 he became the first ever bowler to bowl at over 100mph. Though Shoaib didn't enjoy a very good World Cup in 2003, he is still one of the world's most dangerous and deadly bowlers, as he showed against England at the end of 2005, when he took 17 wickets in three matches and helped Pakistan win the series.

Stumped?

Shoaib's nickname is the Rawalpindi Express?

True or false?

The Stroke Makers

The Cut

The cut is a great stroke to play for any ball that is a little short and wide on the off stump.

But beware! Bowlers often get wickets with bad balls because the batsman is so eager to blast a boundary he loses his concentration. A small 'snick' to the slips and the batsman is walking back to the pavilion. So here is how to cut with confidence!

1

Step back with your rear foot so it is in line with the approaching ball. Your bat should be in a high backlift position and your front shoulder should be pointing towards off-side.

2

Bring the bat down in a 'chopping' motion with your arms fully extended and roll your wrists as you hit the ball so that the ball stays low. Your bottom hand should control the shot. Remember not to lean back!

3

Keep the weight on the back foot and follow through fully with the bat so that it finishes above your head towards off-side.

India's VVS Laxman plays the cut against Australia

Look at the photo of India's fantastic batsman

V V S Laxman cutting the ball for four runs.

Here are five reasons the ball raced to the boundary:

1. He has rolled his wrists to make sure that the ball stays low.

2. His bottom hand is controlling the shot.

3. His head remains still and his eyes are watching the ball.

4. All his weight is on his back foot so that he remains well balanced.

5. His bat has followed through the shot and finished at a high angle.

Warning!

Cutting can lead to catching if you're not careful. So be warned! Don't try to cut a ball that is too close to your body because you'll find yourself leaning back to play the shot – and that's how you edge the ball behind. And if you want to avoid being caught in the covers when you cut, always make sure that the bottom hand controls the shot. If the top hand takes charge, the ball will go up in the air and you'll soon hear a 'Howzat!'

Hotshot:
V V S Laxman nearly gave up cricket to become a doctor.

All-Round Action Heroes

All-rounders can bat with boldness and bowl with brilliance. Cricket is full of these magicians who make double trouble for the opposition!

South Africa's Shaun Pollock is an awesome all-rounder

England's **Andrew Flintoff** is one of the best Test all-rounders, with nearly 200 wickets and 3,000 runs, but other countries have their all-round action heroes too.

South Africa's **Shaun Pollock** has taken over 400 wickets in Test matches and he has a top score with the bat of 111. Teammate **Jacques Kallis** has a batting best of 189 and has taken more than 200 wickets.

Australia's **Andrew Symonds** is a One Day specialist who helped his country win the 2003 World Cup with his spectacular batting and bowling.

New Zealand's **Chris Cairns** has smashed sixes and shattered stumps all over the world!

India's **Ajit Agarkar** took 50 One Day wickets quicker than any other player and, in a match against Zimbabwe in 2000, he belted 50 runs in only 21 balls!

Pakistan have a pair of priceless players in **Shahid Afridi** and **Abdul Razzaq**. In his first ever One Day innings in 1996, Afridi blazed 100 against Sri Lanka in only 37 balls – and he was only 16 at the time! His best bowling figures are a fantastic five wickets for 11 runs.

Razzaq has cracked centuries for Pakistan in Test and One Day matches and he's also taken over 300 international wickets.

The awesome Muttiah Muralitharan in action

HEAVEN'S XI

11

Muttiah Muralitharan
SRI LANKA

Born: April 17 1972 in Kandy, Sri Lanka

● Muttiah Muralitharan played his first Test match for Sri Lanka in 1992 when he was only 20 and, with his amazing spinning style has been taking wickets ever since.

● In March 2004 he became the youngest bowler to take 500 Test wickets and now only Shane Warne of Australia has more wickets than the Sri Lankan off-break bowler.

● 'Murali', as he is known, is just as deadly in One Day Internationals and helped his country win the World Cup for the first time in 1996.

● Against Bangladesh in 2006, he became only the second bowler ever to take 600 wickets in a Test match.

Stumped?

Muttiah Muralitharan took up spin bowling when he was 16 years of age?

True or false?

63

One Day Wonders

Test cricket can be terrific but nothing beats One Day matches for excitement and action.

It's fast, furious and fun, with a white ball used instead of a red one and the players all kitted out in colourful clothes.

The first one day match was held in England in 1962 with each side having 65 overs to score as many runs as possible. In 1971 Australia played England in the first ever One Day International match and four years later the Cricket World Cup was inaugurated.

Now there are hundreds of One Day matches played every year and each country has its own competitions. But what everyone likes best are the international One Day matches, and there have been some thrilling clashes over the years. In March 2006, Australia and South Africa scored 872 runs between them in one of the most exciting One Day matches ever.

Pakistan's Inzamam-ul-Haq is a One Day wonder

Stumped Solutions

1. Trescothick - False
2. Smith - True
3. Ponting - True
4. Tenulkar - True
5. Lara - True
6. Pietersen - True
7. Flintoff - False
8. Gilchrist - False
9. Warne - True
10. Akhtar - True
11. Muralitharan - False